P9-BYM-262

My WONDERFUL WORLD of SHOES

Nina Chakrabarti

LAURENCE KING PUBLISHING

LAURENCE KING

PUBLISHED IN 2012 BY
LAURENCE KING PUBLISHING LTD
361-373 CITY ROAD
LONDON EC1V 1LR
TEL + 44 20 7841 6900
FAX + 44 20 7841 6910
E-mail : enquiries@laurenceking.com
www.laurenceking.com

© 2012 NINA CHAKRABARTI

NINA CHAKRABARTI HAS ASSERTED HER RIGHT
UNDER THE COPYRIGHT, DESIGNS, AND PATENT ACT
1988 TO BE IDENTIFIED AS THE AUTHOR OF THIS WORK.

ALL RIGHTS RESERVED. NO PART OF THIS PUBLICATION MAY BE
REPRODUCED OR TRANSMITTED IN ANY FORM OR BY ANY MEANS,
ELECTRONIC OR MECHANICAL, INCLUDING PHOTOCOPY,
RECORDING OR ANY INFORMATION STORAGE AND
RETRIEVAL SYSTEM, WITHOUT PRIOR PERMISSION IN
WRITING FROM THE PUBLISHER.

A CATALOGUE RECORD FOR THIS BOOK IS AVAILABLE
FROM THE BRITISH LIBRARY

ISBN- 978 1 78067 001 0

PRINTED IN CHINA

GIVE A GIRL the RIGHT SHOES, and
SHE CAN CONQUER THE WORLD

— Marilyn Monroe

English flower-patterned shoes from the 1800s

Louis heel named after King Louis XIV of France

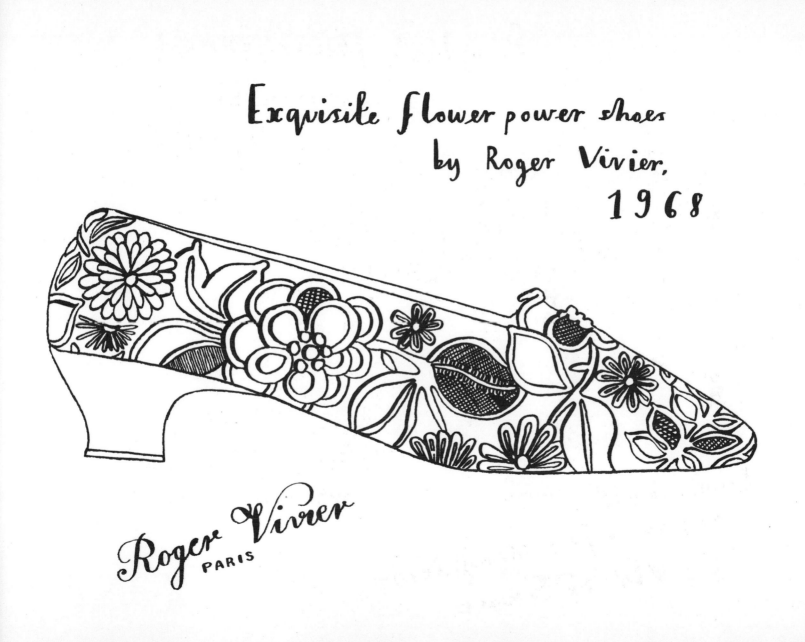

Exquisite flower power shoes
by Roger Vivier,
1968

Roger Vivier PARIS

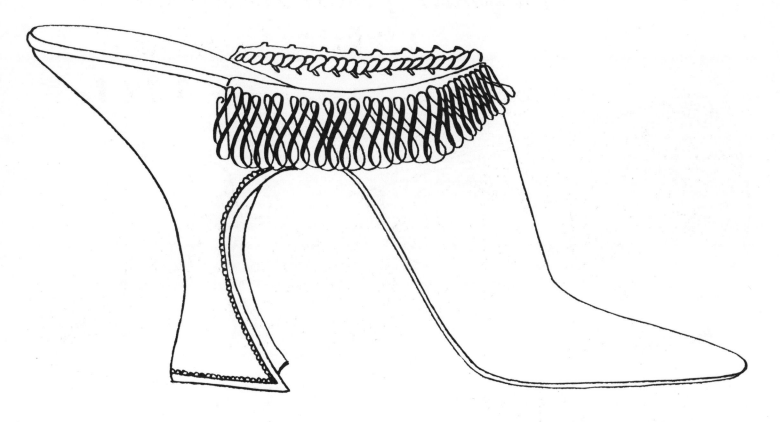

1780's court shoe

1980's court shoe

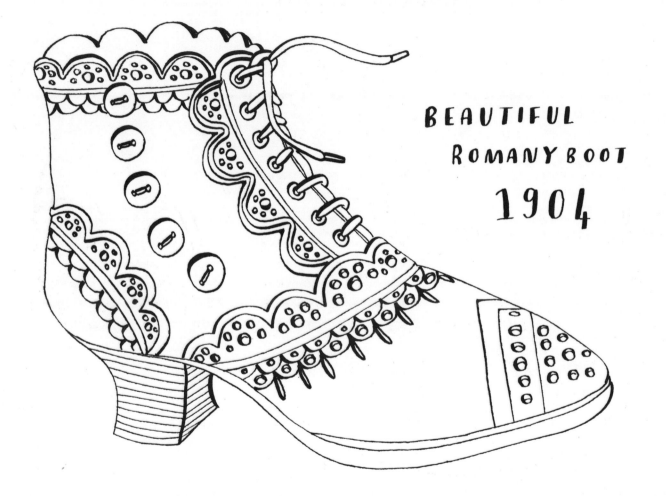

BEAUTIFUL
ROMANY BOOT
1904

Steven Arpad

1930's

BOOT

Made in France

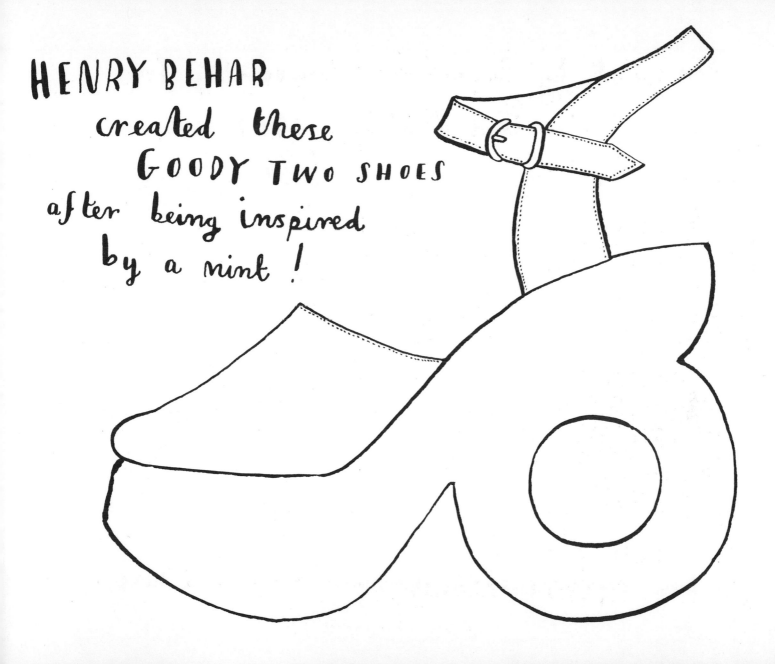

HENRY BEHAR created these GOODY TWO SHOES after being inspired by a mint !

Designed by Roger Vivier especially for
Marlene Dietrich, 1967

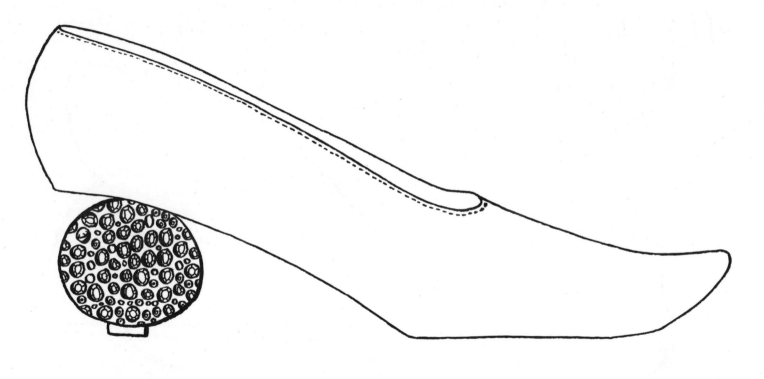

The opulence of a 'diamond'-encrusted heel

The NO HEEL shoe

Elegant 1950's court shoes

colour each check a different colour

I imagine Marilyn Monroe wearing these shoes

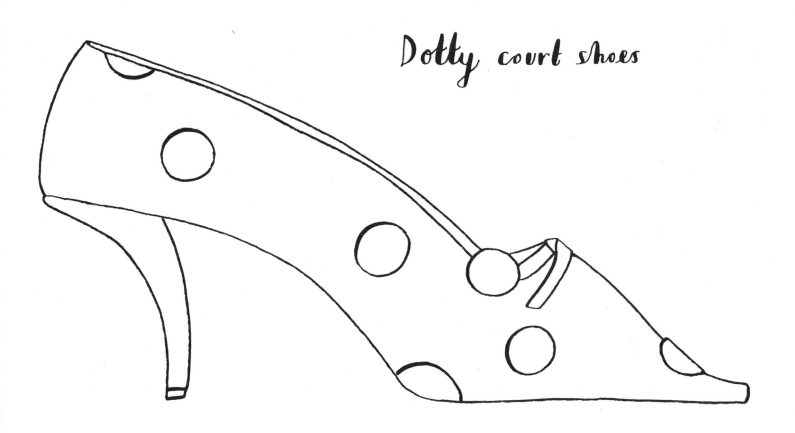

Dotty court shoes

Who can you imagine wearing these?

Shoes depicting the African Savannah

HOW AMAZING!

Shoe depicting a peacock

HOW ELEGANT !

MODERNIST MARVEL

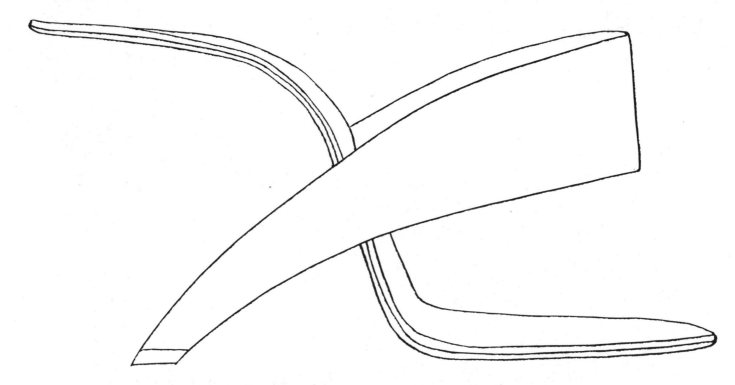

Decorative darling

Designed to prevent wooden floors getting ruined by stiletto heels

GINA's wheel heel shoes

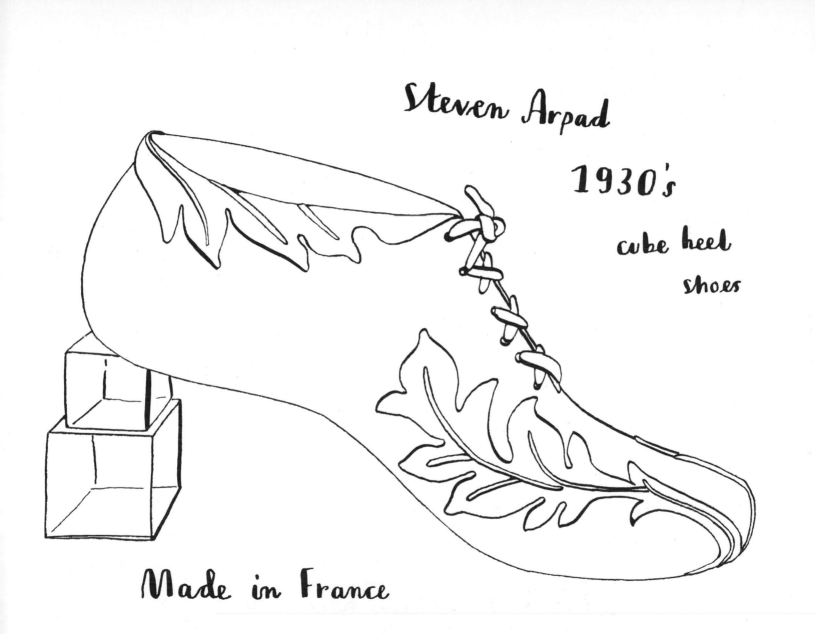

Steven Arpad

1930's

cube heel

shoes

Made in France

André Perugia

1930s

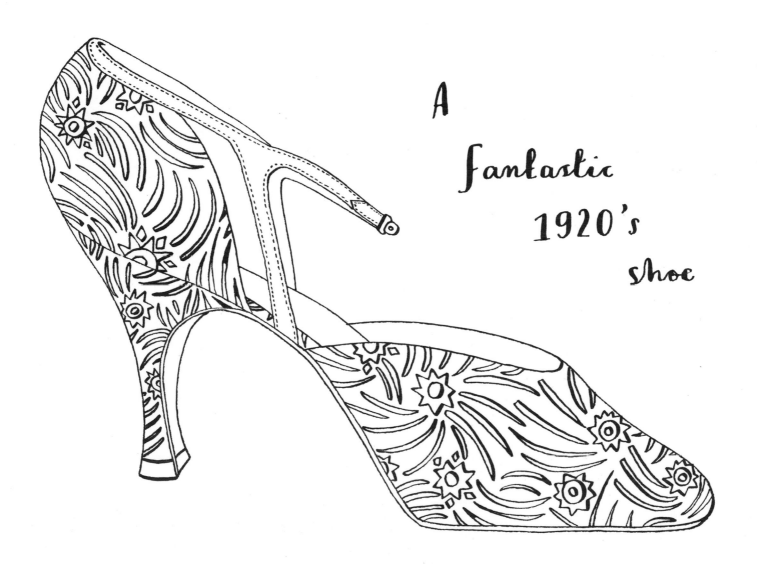

A
fantastic
1920's
shoe

1920's
BOOTIES

Colour with pleasure

Colour brown, pink and red

1800's
BOOTIES

Chez Bremmel

BOTTIER

197, Promenade des Anglais – NICE

FASHION
GIRL ©
MADE IN ITALY

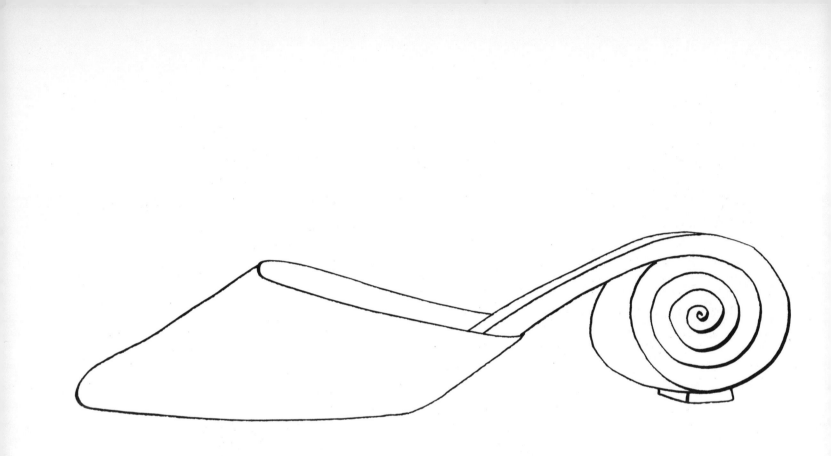

Beth and Herbert Levine, 1954

Andrea Pfister,
1994

MAUD FRIZON

PARIS

Made in
GREAT BRITAIN
by
Chelsea Cobbler
1971

Twinkle twinkle
little shoe...

Made by
Cooch of London,
1860

1960's
Flowery pumps

Shoe la la

Cover this shoe with gold glitter and sequins

MIU MIU, 2011

Made in Italy

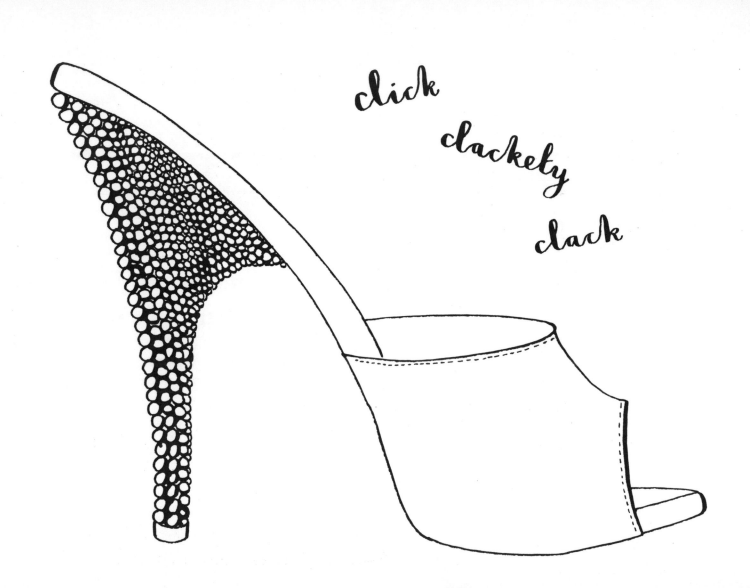

click clackety clack

Bling

ting

a

ling

marouf BOTTIER

Paint each sequin a different colour

Cover this shoe
with hundreds of
beautiful sequins

Designed for
the film Cleopatra 1934

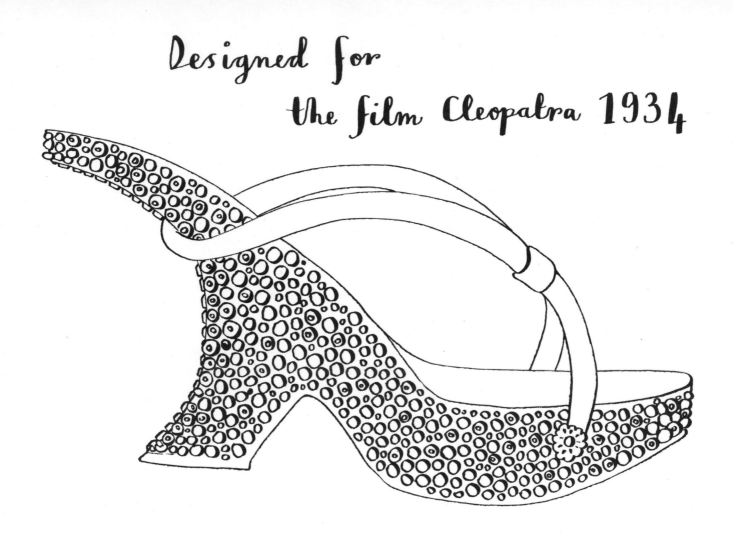

Colour each gem a different spectacular colour

Cover the heel
with
precious gems

Make them sparkle and shine!

A European mule from the 1900s

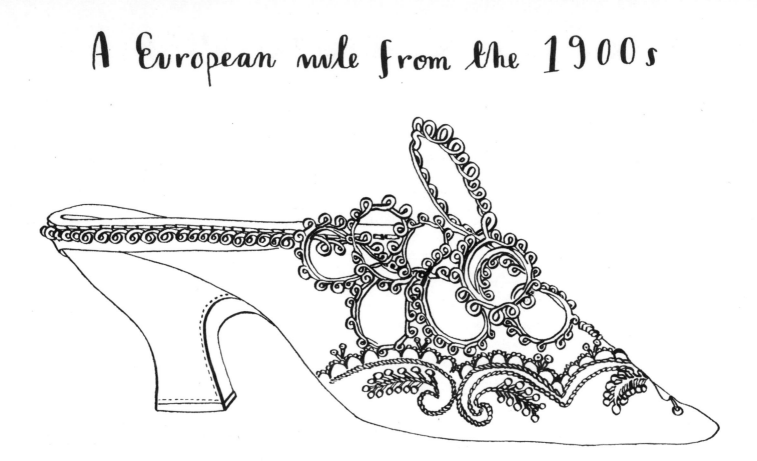

A mule is a backless shoe with a closed toe

A Stingback shoe from the 1950s

A stingback is a backless shoe
with a strap behind the ankle

Shoe be do be do...

From the boutique label

ALBANESE of ROME

Made in the 1950s

1920's velvet shoe

Fill this shoe with an amazing pattern and stunning colours

Made in China
1870 – 1900

Designed by

BEVERLY FELDMAN
1980s

Dolcis

MADE IN U.S.A.

Boudoir Model

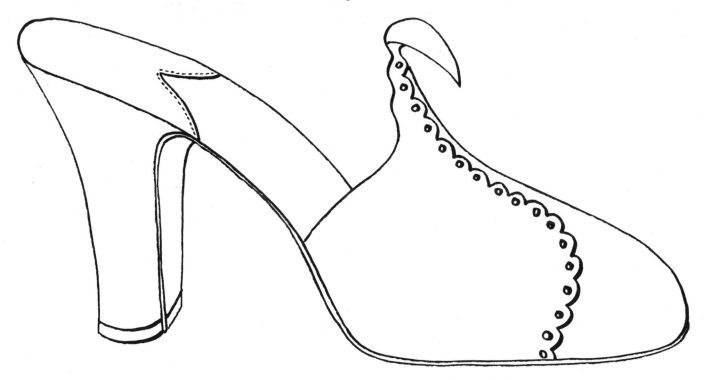

Manchu lady's shoe

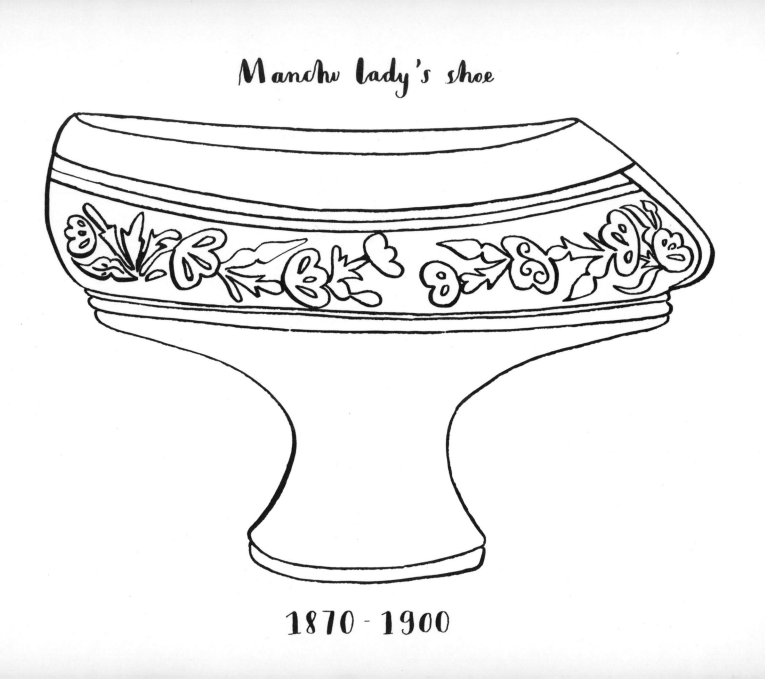

1870 - 1900

KABUKI PUMPS

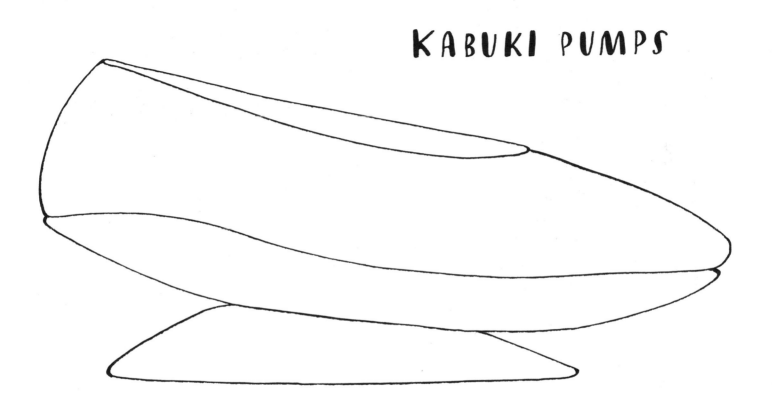

Designed by Beth Levine, 1964

German
half-boot, 1830

Invent a pattern for this
minimalist shoe

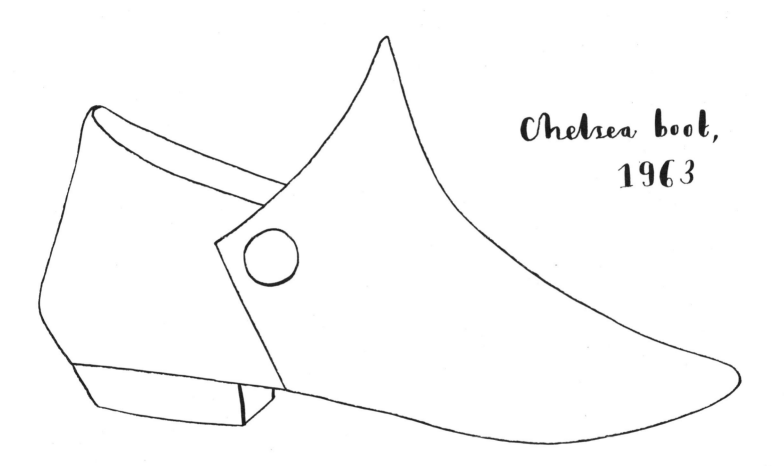

Chelsea boot,
1963

Made in England

Salvatore Ferragamo 1943

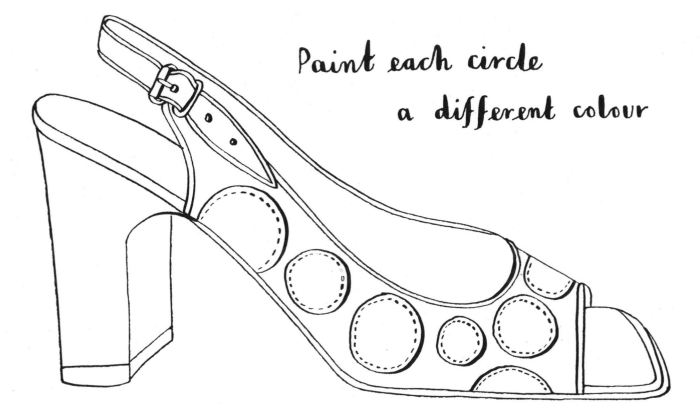

Paint each circle
a different colour

Colour the triangles
gold and black

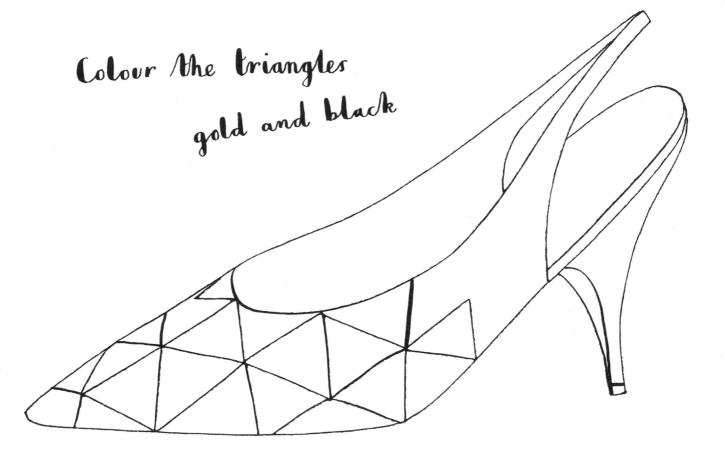

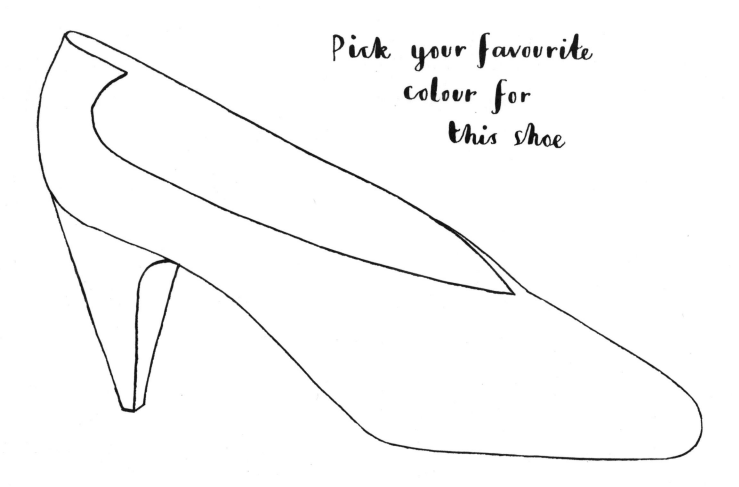

Pick your favourite
colour for
this shoe

USE your
orange, pink,
green and blue pens
for this beautiful shoe

ENZO
OF
ROMA

Bunny shoe

Mouse shoe

SQUEAK!

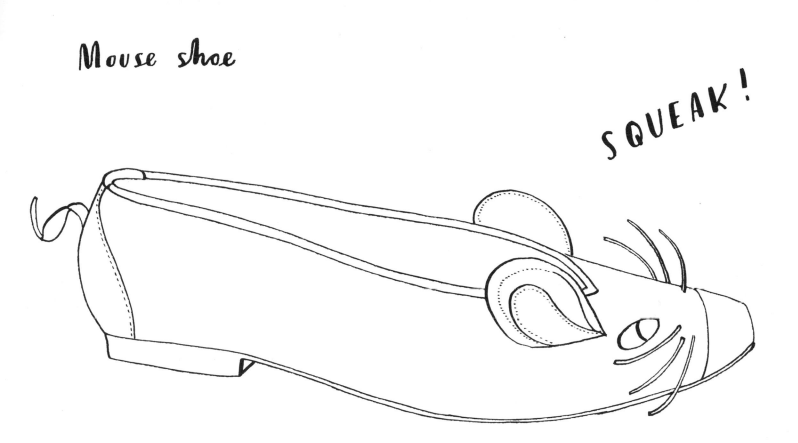

ENZO
OF
ROMA

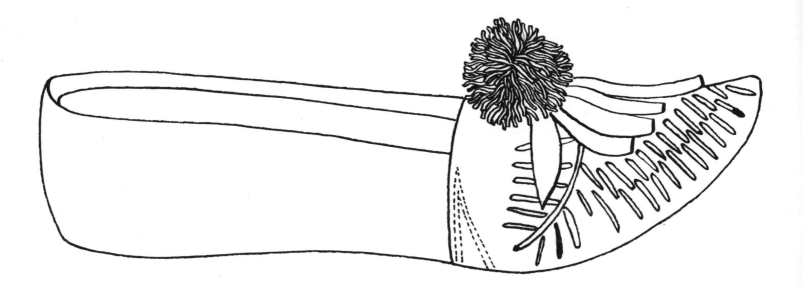

Native American Loafers, 1900s

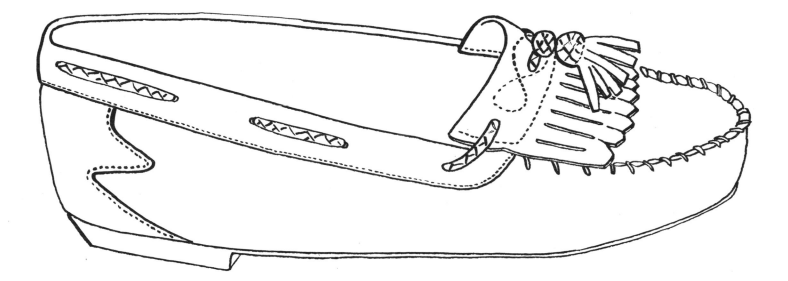

Brazilian loafers, 1970s

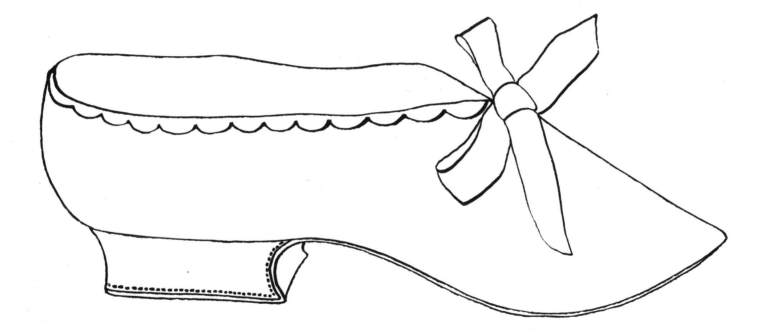

Angular shapes rule
in this
ANDRÉ PERUGIA
creation

Curls curl up
to create the
heel in this
decorative marvel

Embroidered Manchu platform shoes

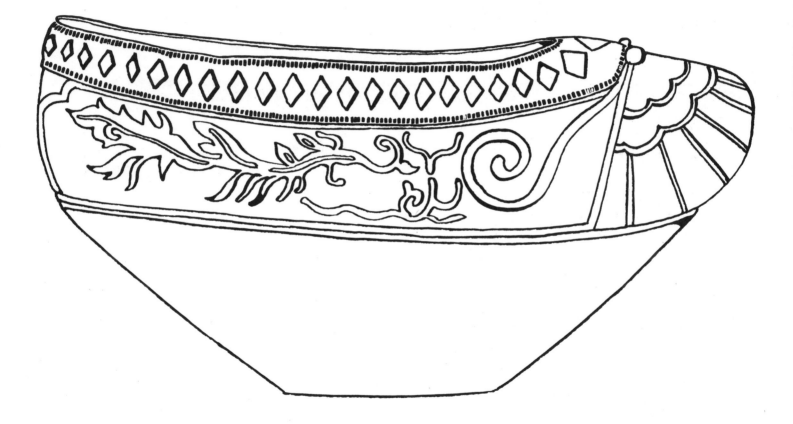

MADE IN CHINA, 1894

1990
Jean Paul Gaultier

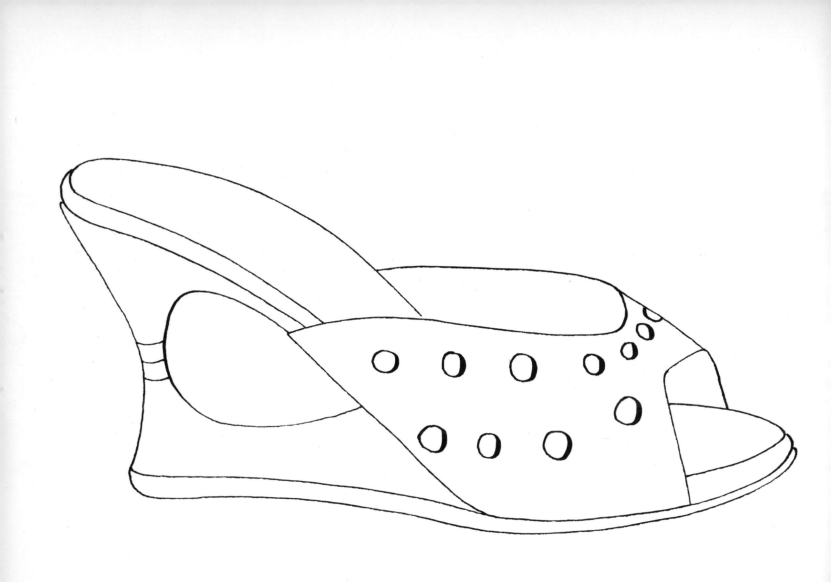

MAISON
MARTIN
MARGIELA

Split-toe
TABI
boots

From the city of LOS ANGELES
comes the split-sole
JEFFREY
CAMPBELL
shoe

Inspired by the Beatles song —
I'm Looking Through You
1973, Jan Jansen

Metallic sandals

LUNA

Designed by
Camille Unglik

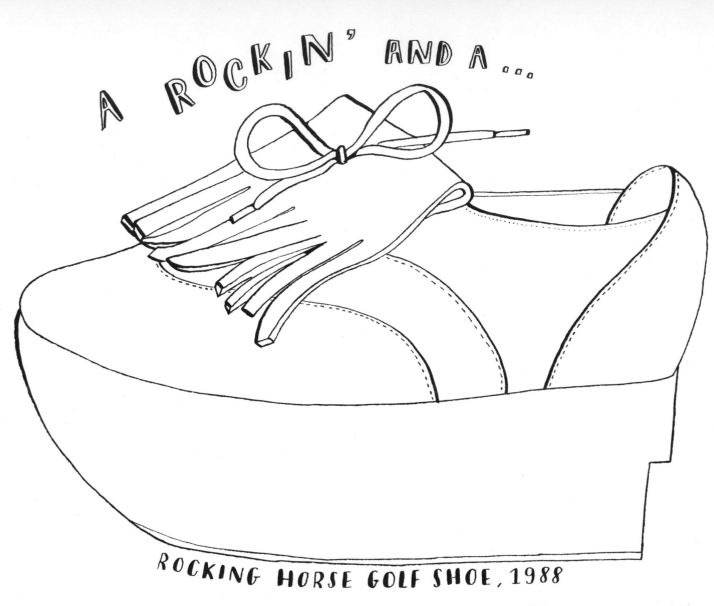

A ROCKIN' AND A ...

ROCKING HORSE GOLF SHOE, 1988

Vivienne Westwood

Get busy with your pattern making skills with these wedge boots

OOH Mama Jama

1972 CLOGS

Best not run for the bus in these

NEW YORK · PARIS · ALBUQUERQUE

Rhinestone beauty

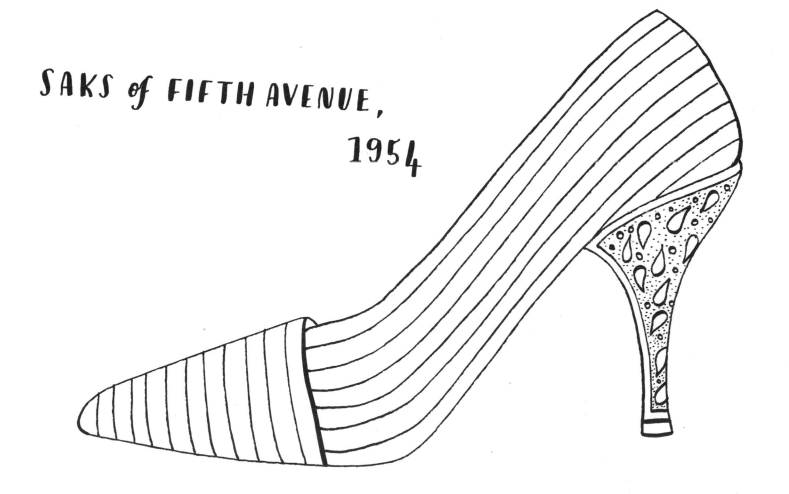

SAKS *of* FIFTH AVENUE,
1954

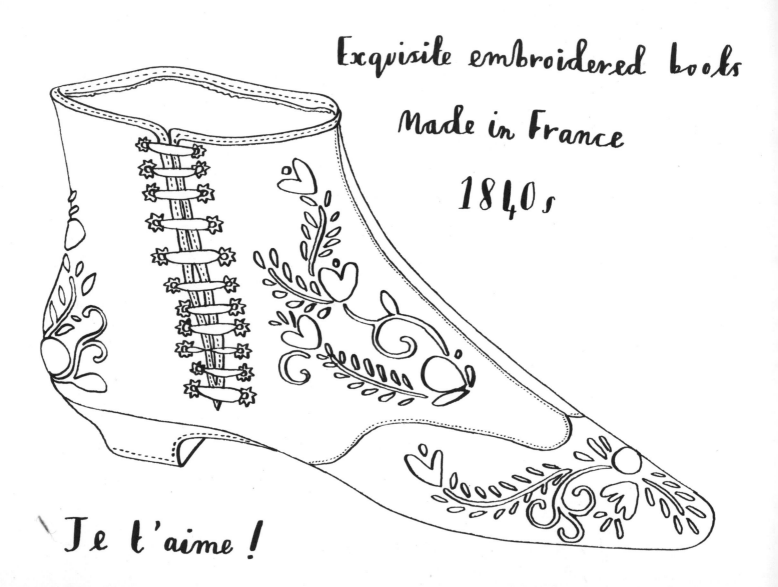

Exquisite embroidered boots
Made in France
1840s

Je t'aime !

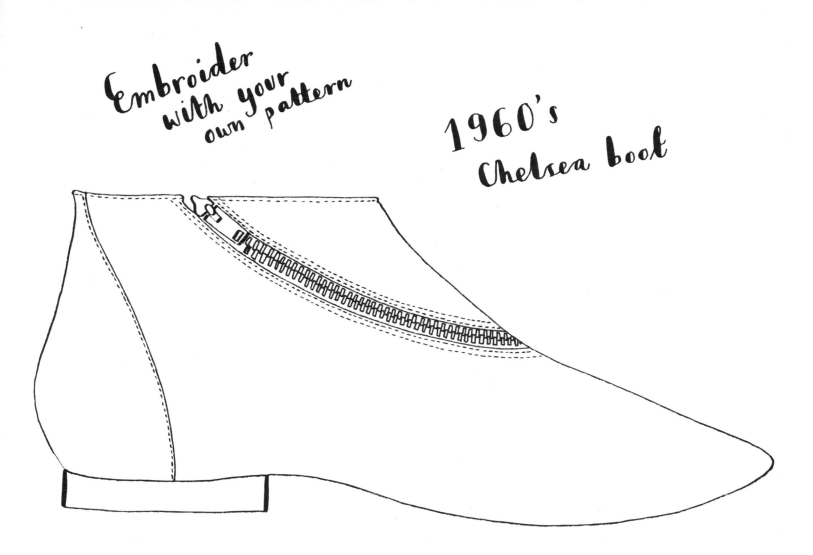

Embroider with your own pattern

1960's Chelsea boot

Zip-e-dee doo dah...

Jelly shoes
became popular in the 1980s

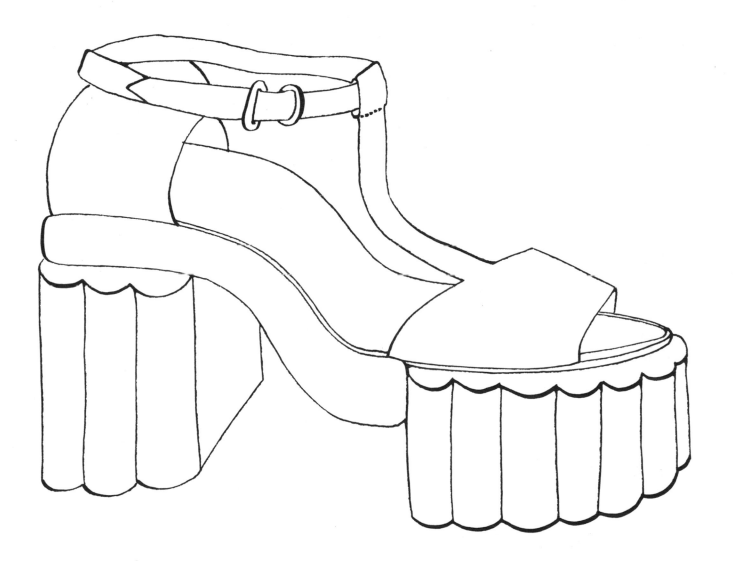

Made in Canada

Incredible
1970's platform sandals

1970's
Peep Toe
platform Sandals

Made in the U.S. of A.

ROGER VIVIER shoes

Colour the bows orange

The bow transforms this shoe into something really special

Inspired by
18th-century snuff boxes

Oxford lace-ups,
Beth Levine
1970

Super elegant
OXFORDS

The marvellous
'HUG MY LEG' shoes
Designed by Jan Jansen

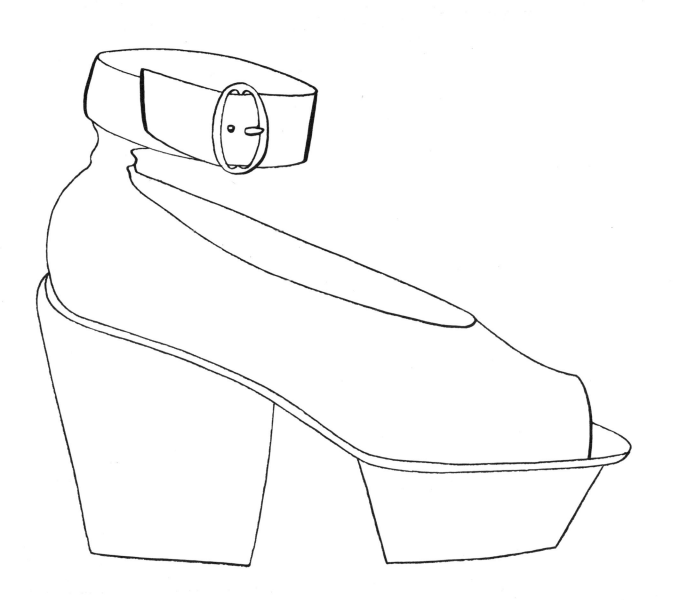

Paint each circle
a different colour

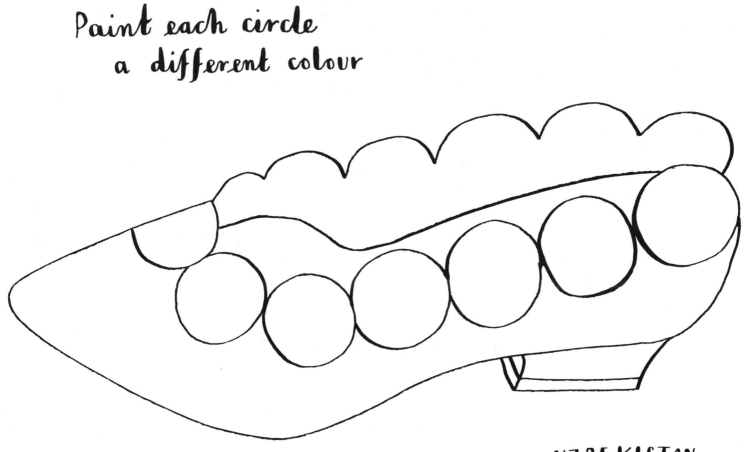

MADE in UZBEKISTAN
1989

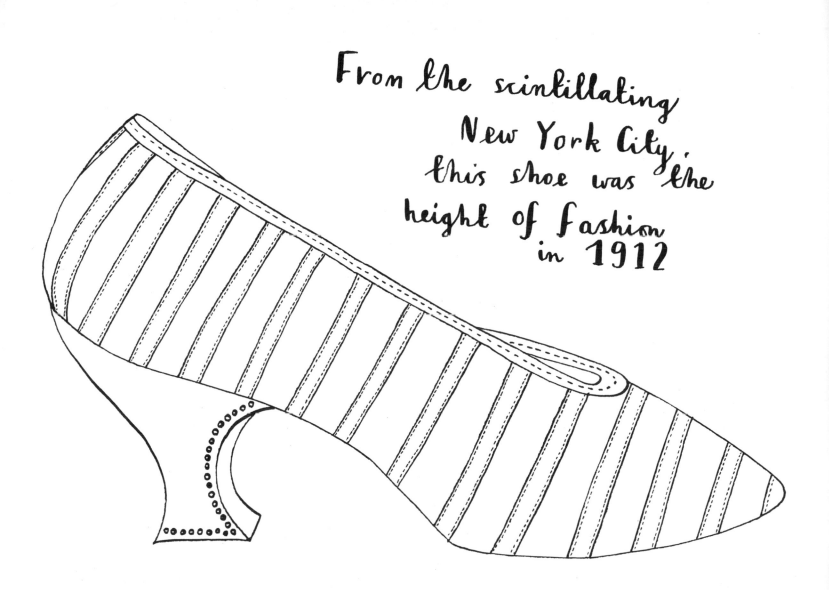

From the scintillating
New York City,
this shoe was the
height of fashion
in 1912

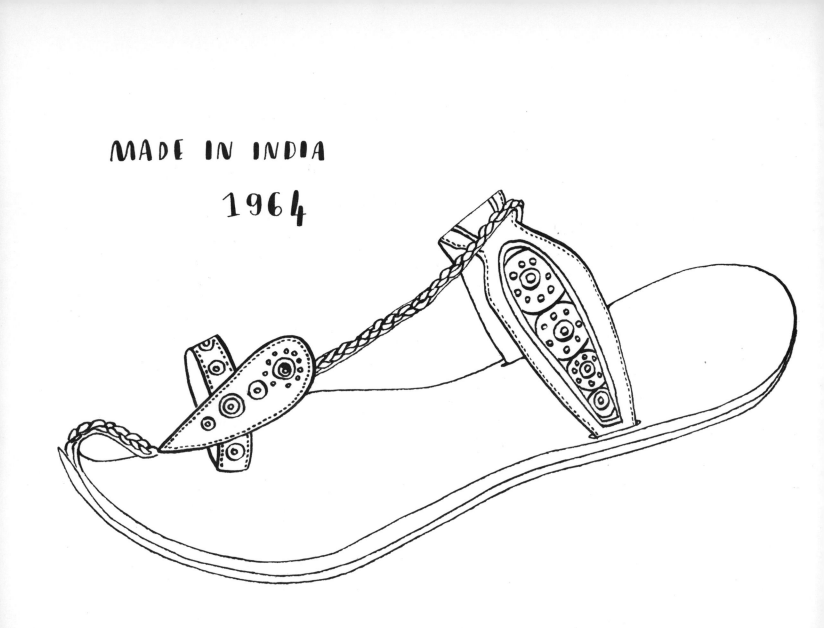

MADE IN INDIA

1964

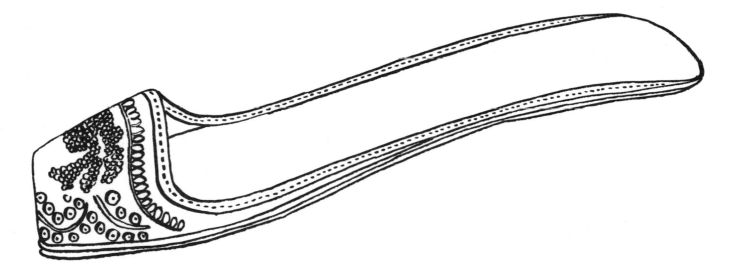

MADE IN VIETNAM

early 20th century

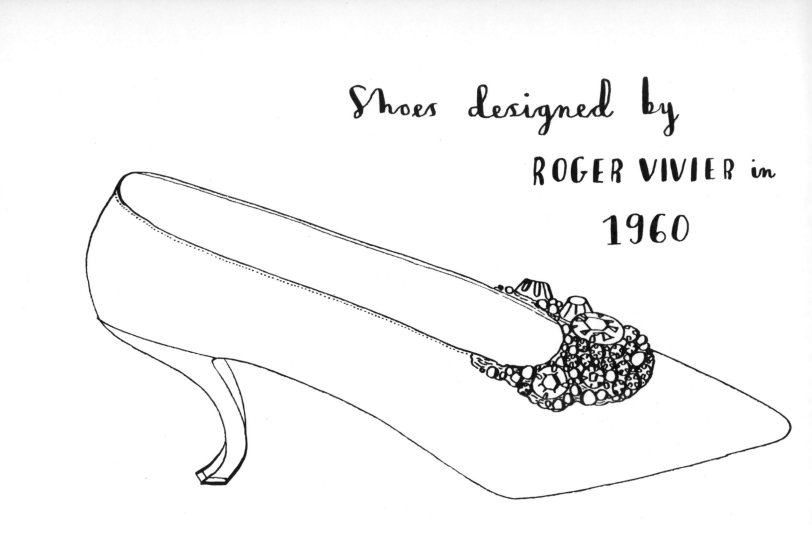

Shoes designed by ROGER VIVIER in 1960

He invented the COMMA heel

In America,
    the winkle-picker
was called the
            NEEDLE NEEDLE

Shoe le taxi

Margaret Jerrold

This shoe features the New York skyline

My little town blues are melting away...

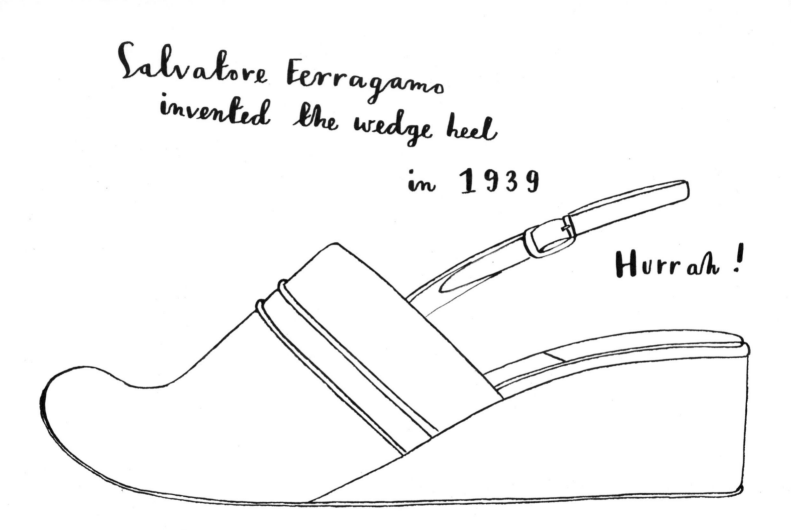

Salvatore Ferragamo
invented the wedge heel

in 1939

Hurrah!

Peep Toe wedges

Made in Taiwan

1973

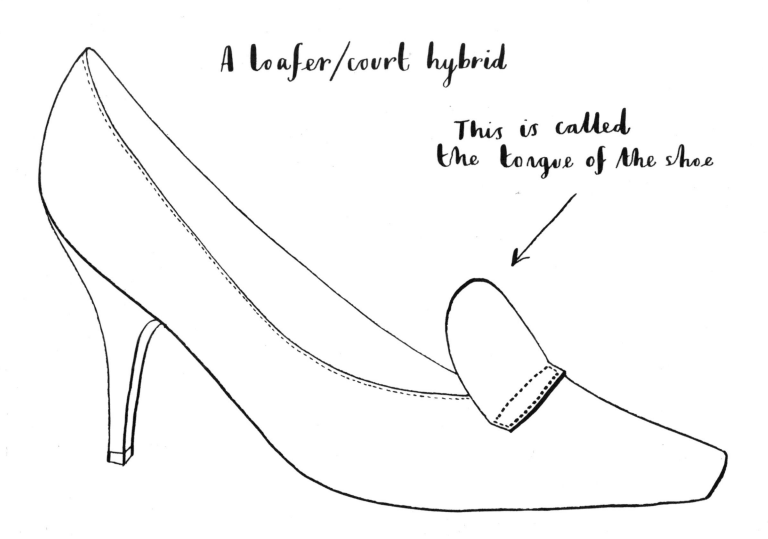

A loafer/court hybrid

This is called
the tongue of the shoe

Create a marvellous pattern

for this loafer

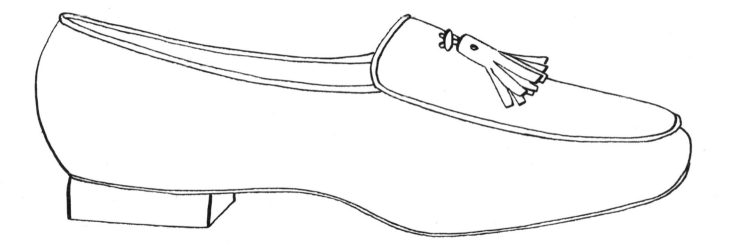

It's grand being tall  sometimes

'scuse me
while I kiss
the
sky

U.S.A.
1930

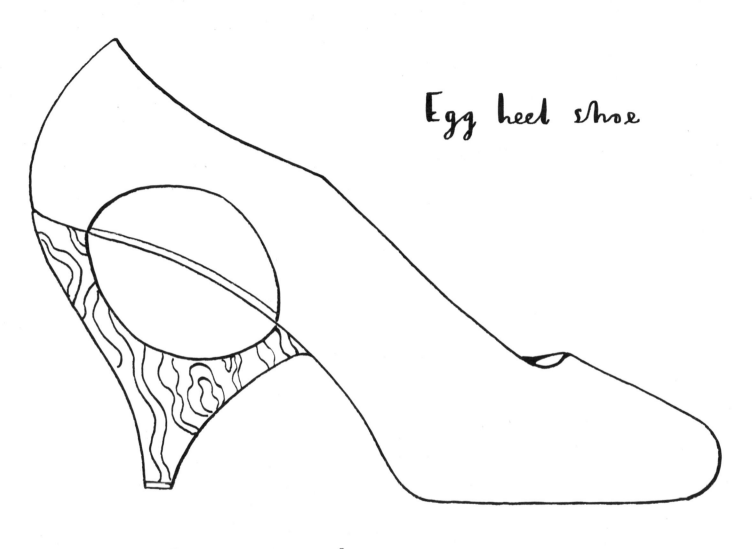

Egg heel shoe

Christian Louboutin, 1988

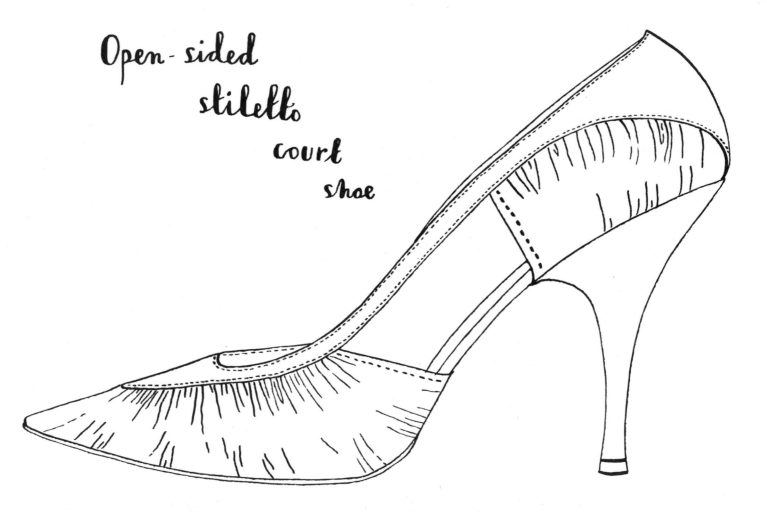

Open-sided
stiletto
court
shoe

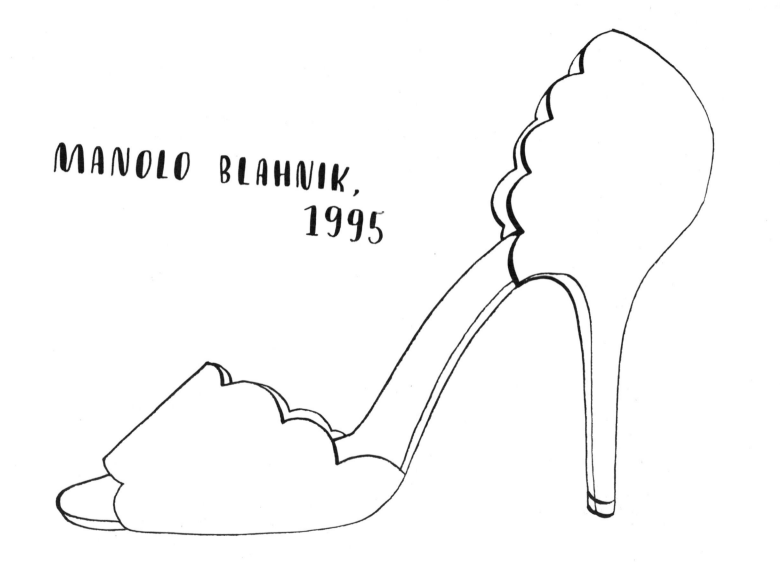

MANOLO BLAHNIK,
1995

Put the blame on Mame, boys
Put the blame on Mame

(especially if she wears shoes like these)

Salvatore Ferragamo
wedge heels
1938

Made in Italy

Regulation wartime shoes

CC41

Colour each
button
carefully and
with love

Paint each
flower a
beautiful colour

Terry de Havilland
1998

Colour the heart red

Paint a psychedelic pattern, onto these sculptural wooden platforms

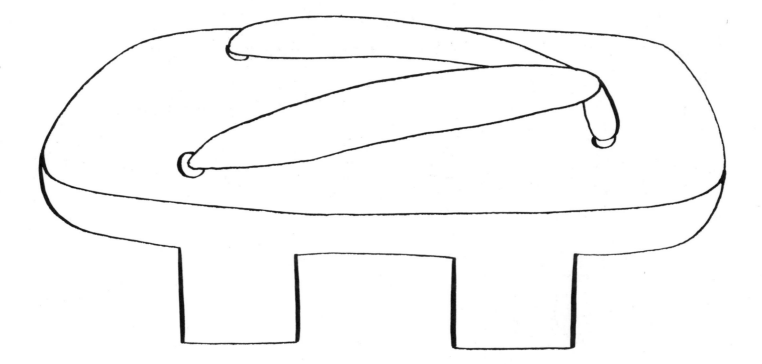

Made in JAPAN

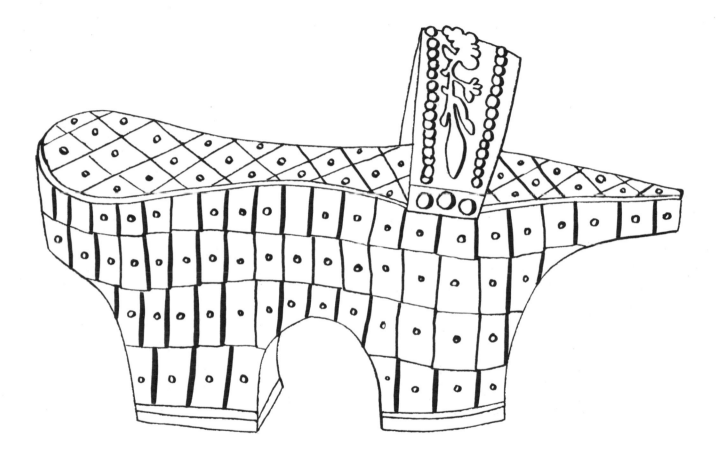

Made in TUNISIA

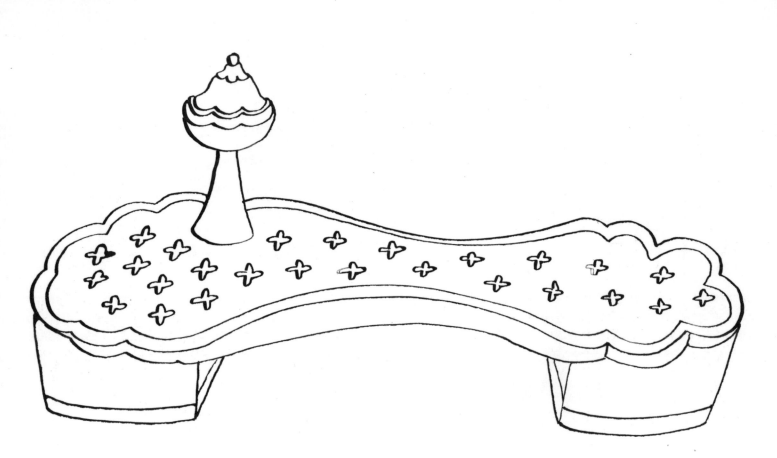

19th-century Indian toe-knob sandal

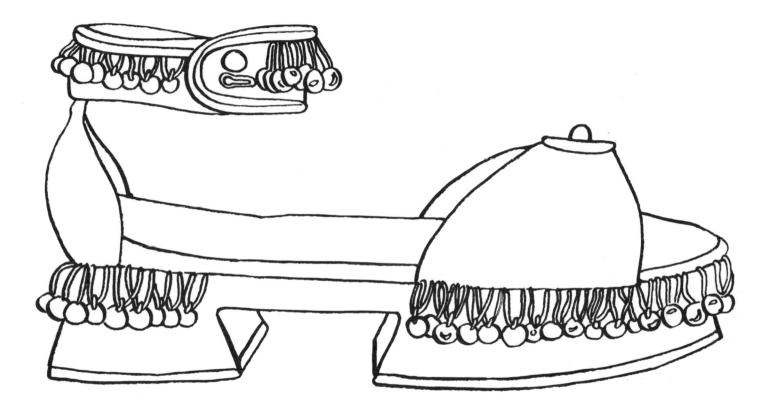

20th- century Puerto Rican sandal

A high-heeled
shoe with
brogue detailing

O beautiful brogue
I love thee

The inverted heel

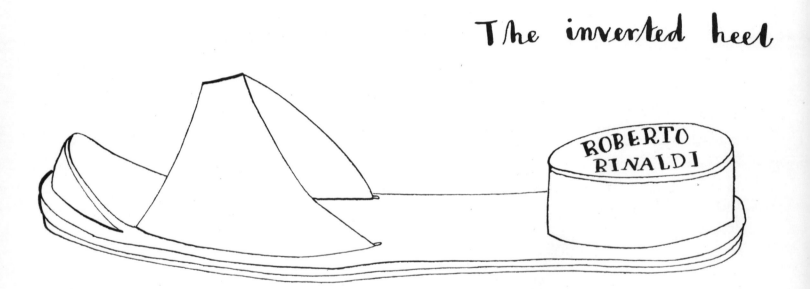

ROBERTO
RINALDI

Roberto Rinaldi, 2007

The very peculiar heel

Traditional Greek shoes

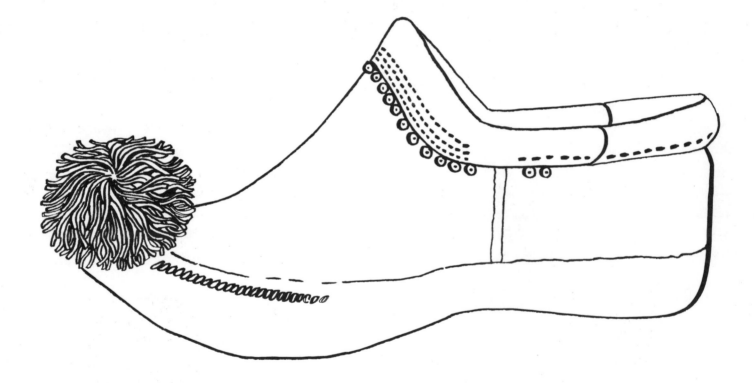

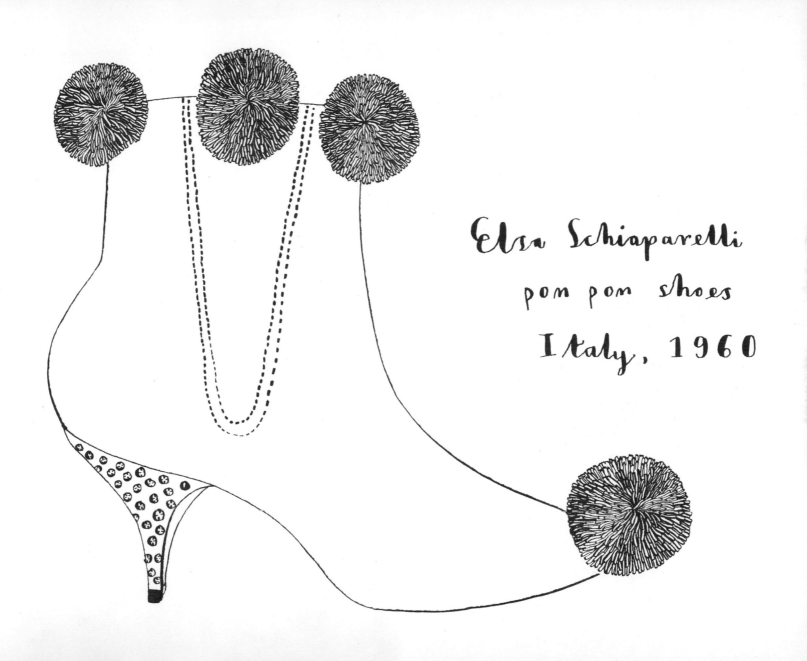

Elsa Schiaparelli
pon pon shoes
Italy, 1960

P✹P art shoe

Vivienne Westwood

Credits

ALBANESE OF ROME – www.albaneseroma.com

BEVERLY FELDMAN – www.beverlyfeldmanshoes.com

CHRISTIAN LOUBOUTIN – www.christianlouboutin.com

GINA – www.gina.com
Designed by Mehmet Kurdash of GINA shoes

JAN JANSEN – www.janjansenshoes.com

JEFFREY CAMPBELL – www.jeffreycampbellshoes.com

MANOLO BLAHNIK – www.manoloblahnik.com

MAISON MARTIN MARGIELA – www.maisonmartinmargiela.com

MIU MIU – www.miumiu.com

NINA – www.ninashoes.com

ROGER VIVIER – www.rogervivier.com

SALVATORE FERRAGAMO – www.ferragamo.com

TERRY DE HAVILLAND – www.tdhcouture.com

ELSA SCHIAPARELLI – www.schiaparelli.com

JEAN PAUL GAULTIER – www.jeanpaulgaultier.com

MAUD FRIZON – www.maudfrizon.com

VIVIENNE WESTWOOD – www.viviennewestwood.co.uk
Rocking Horse Golf Shoe, 1988 & Can Shoe, 2005

THANK YOU!

LAURENCE KING, JO LIGHTFOOT, ANGUS HYLAND,
IDA RIVEROS, MELISSA DANNY, FELICITY AWDRY,
GIOVANNA CELLINI, CLARE PRICE, LAURA CARLIN,
THE ROYAL COLLEGE OF ART LIBRARY,
ALLY WALLER, CLARE SHILLAND,
ZACHARY BREDEMEAR,
and
BEN BRANAGAN